AN AMERICAN
REVOLUTION OF 2008

AN
AMERICAN
REVOLUTION OF 2008

The Campaign and Election of
President BARACK OBAMA

H. MARCEL EVANS

authorHOUSE®

AuthorHouse™
1663 Liberty Drive
Bloomington, IN 47403
www.authorhouse.com
Phone: 1-800-839-8640

First published by AuthorHouse   11/10/2011

ISBN: 978-1-4670-3367-1 (sc)
ISBN: 978-1-4670-3368-8 (ebk)

Library of Congress Control Number: 2011916227

Printed in the United States of America

Any people depicted in stock imagery provided by Thinkstock are models, and such images are being used for illustrative purposes only.

Certain stock imagery © Thinkstock.

This book is printed on acid-free paper.

Preface

I am aware that there have been improvements made in Race Relations in America over the past twenty years. I worked in an area of Race Relations in the military in the 1970s. I did not think I would see an African American be elected as president of the United States in my lifetime. I was very excited prior to the election, at the possibility of Mr. Obama being elected to be president. I wanted to be sure that I was able to vote. As fate would have it, I was scheduled for an operation on Election Day. My wife checked and found a place where we could vote absentee ballot.

My operation was done and Mr. Obama was elected. I had an extensive recovery period, and somehow began to think of Mr. Obama's campaign as a revolution of words and ideas of change. I then decided that after my rehabilitation period I would document some of the events during the campaign, and after Mr. Obama's election I wanted to show that some of his campaign promises and ideas were truly revolutionary. So I thought, why not call the campaign and election an American Revolution of 2008?

Acknowledgements

First I must thank God from whom all blessings flow. I thank God for all the blessings in my life and for the courage to face things that some times seem impossible.

I thank my parents who really taught me about unconditional love, honesty, and the value of family.

I am very grateful for my wife Zenobia, whom I knew from the first time I saw her, she was the person I wanted to be with. She has always supported me throughout the many years of our marriage, in all areas. She is the one person I can truly trust and depend on, and she is truly the greatest pleasure of my life.

After my wife, the next most valuable people in my life are my children: Marceles, Robin, Randall, Ronda, Rami, and Andre.

From my children, I have been blessed with six granddaughters: Ayana, Ante, Aliyah, Ayia and twins Katrina and Kloe.

I must give a special thanks to my daughter Ronda who was very helpful in assisting me with the preparation of this writing.

Thanks also to my daughter-in-law Deborah who helped me with a previous work. I would like to thank all the members of my extended family and the many close friends we have, Thank you all for being a part of my life experience.

Events in 2009

January 2009

May 1, 2009	Need for Health Care Reform
May 1, 2009	President Obama Nominates Judge Sotomayor for the Supreme Court
June 25, 2009	Role of First Lady
December 23, 2009	First Year Recovery/ Economy Health Care Bill
December 25, 2009	Health Care Legislation Approved Christmas Eve

Events of 2010

January 20, 2010	Election of Scott Brown (Edward Kennedy's Vacancy) Martha Coakley was Democratic Candidate
January 20, 2010	20 Yr. Old From Bethesda, MD 61 Month Jail Term for Plot to Kill President Obama
April 23, 2010	President Obama to New York Meet w / Financial Exc.—Financial Reform
April 23, 2010	Speech on Financial Sector
May 10, 2010	Selection of Elena Kagan Supreme Court
June 21, 2010	President Obama— Ref. Fathers for Father's Day

June 22, 2010	President Obama Met with Insurance Exc. Of Major Insurance Companies Ref. Raising Premiums
June 23, 2010	Problems with Combat in Afghan.—Talk of Possibility of General Stanley McChrystal being fired
August 7, 2010	Ref. Stimulus Pkg.
August 7, 2010	Ref. American Health Ins.
August 11, 2010	
August 18, 2010	Some of President Obama's Promises Coming to Pass Week of August 19, 2010
August 31, 2010	President Eco. Team Discussing Ways to Bolster Growths and Improve Job Opportunities
August 31, 2010	President Obama Declares U.S. War in Iraq Over
September 1, 2010	Iraq War Over
September 22, 2010	Ref. Bob Woodward's Book—Way Out of Afghanistan in 2009
October 8, 2010	Ref. Federal Workers—Working at Home
November 3, 2010	Midterm Election Very Difficult for President Obama and Democrats

November 14, 2010	Ref. President Obama Being a One-Term President
December 1, 2010	Mtg. President Obama and Republicans to Reach Agreement on the Tax Cuts Due to Expire End of 2010
December 1, 2010	Another Campaign Promise was to Repeal the Policy "Don't Ask Don't Tell"
December 3, 2010	Ref. Tax Cuts
December 3, 2010	Mrs. Obama Greeting Injured Service Members and Their Families
December 7, 2010	President Willing to Compromise
December 17, 2010	
December 18, 2010	Don't Ask Don't Tell
December 19, 2010	
December 23, 2010	
December 31, 2010	Financial Crisis Began on Wall Street—Risky Mortgages, etc.
December 31, 2010	Eco Growth

Events of 2011

January 6, 2011	Harry Reid (D-Nev.) still Leaderof Senate
January 6, 2011	Republicans Gain Control of the House of Representatives

This writing is an attempt to show Barack Obama's campaign as an American Political Revolution. Revolutions of the past had battles of various types. Obama's 2008 campaign was a revolution with battles of words, ideas and strategies. His major theme was there is a need for change in the federal government in some areas.

According to Webster's New Collegiate Dictionary, the definition of revolution is—activity or movement designed to affect fundamental changes in the socioeconomic situation of a country.

Most leaders of revolutions seem to have a background that prepares them for the revolution they have been chosen to lead.

In 1961 Barack Obama was born in Hawaii to mixed parents, a white teenage mother and a black African father. Two years after Obama's birth his parents were divorced because the father had left his family. His mother married a student from Indonesia. They moved to Jakarta in 1967. In 1971 Obama moved back to Hoululu, Hawaii, to live with his grandparents, a white couple from Kansas. He attended Punahou, a college prep school. His grandparents were a very important part of his preparation to lead the American Revolution of 2008. It provided him another form of insight in his relationships with people of different backgrounds.

Barack Obama was born on August 4, 1961. That time period was a very turbulent time for race relations in the United States. On August 4,

1961 in Alabama and Mississippi, voting officials imposed rigid standards on black applicants. In New Orleans on August 4, 1961, there was an expulsion of six black students from Alabama State College. The students had staged a sit-in at the Montgomery County Courthouse lunch grill. Black Americans were not allowed to eat there.

In Washington, security police had arrested five blacks for trying to integrate the Glen Echo Amusement Park in Maryland. The blacks were asking the U.S. Supreme Court to review the case.

There was an incident in Shreveport, LA on August 4, 1961. Black people were not allowed to enter the waiting room of the Trailway bus depot. State and local laws prohibited black people from entering a waiting room for whites only.

On that day four Freedom Riders attempted to enter the waiting room and were arrested for disturbing the peace. Two compatriots were also arrested, accused of encouraging the Freedom Riders.

The National Voting Rights Act of 1965 received final approval from the Senate on August 4. The measure was signed two days later by President Johnson.

There are many things that made Obama a pleasing personality to so many people of different backgrounds. Working as a community organizer helped him form a good relationship with people at the grass root level. I am sure there were other career opportunities available to him, but he seemed to know just what he needed to do in preparation for his goal of becoming president of the United States.

Much of his background is a reflection of many situations that exist in our society. Maybe this is why so many people find Obama so appealing. They can relate to one or more events in his background. Many voters sometimes complained that most politicians cannot possibly understand their problems, but maybe this guy Obama does. In many cases he not only understood the problem, he had lived it, or knew someone who had.

In 1979 Obama began his first year at Occidental College, in Los Angeles. He transferred to Columbia University in New York after his sophomore year at Occidental College. Obama graduated from Columbia in 1983, and became a Community Organizer in Chicago. He entered Harvard Law School in 1988 and became President of its law review. After graduating magna cum laude from Harvard Law School, he returned to Chicago to begin a career as a civil rights lawyer.

Obama met Michelle Robinson in 1989 during a summer internship in Chicago and they were married in 1992.

1993—Obama joins the Law Firm of Mines, Barnhill & Galland of Chicago Law School.

1995—Publishes Dreams from my Father, a New York Times best seller.

1996—Obama entered elective politics and was elected to his first term as an Illinois State Senator.

He was also elected to the Illinois Senate in 1996. Alice Palmer, the incumbent from his district, failed to get the required number of signatures to get back in the race. This made it possible for Obama to get elected.

2003—Obama began his U.S. Senate Campaign in January 2003. He drove from Springfield to Rockford for a banquet honoring black and Hispanic professionals and was not called on to speak, instead had to sit at a back table as a motivational speaker.

In the 2004 U.S. Senate Race, Obama defeated Alan Keyes, a former presidential candidate by the largest electoral victory in Illinois history. After being elected to the U.S. Senate on November 2, 2004, Obama became the fifth African American U.S. Senator in American history.

27 July 2004—Obama was chosen to deliver the keynote address at the 2004 Democratic National Convention in Boston. This was a surprise because he was unknown outside of his home state. Keynote speaker Obama stated,

> "There is not a liberal America and a conservative America—there is the United States of America. There is not a black America and a white America and a Latino America and Asian America—there is the United States of America."

2005—Named one of the World's most influential people by *Time Magazine.*

Most candidates did not consider Obama a threat, because he was so new to politics and not very much experience. There was also the fact, that he was an African American. Many Americans did not believe that an African American could be elected to be president in 2008.

2006—Obama was on a tour in Africa to raise awareness about HIV/AIDS. He also visited Kenya, his father's homeland. He also published The Audacity of Hope in 2006.

In the United States of America, there are two major parties, the Democratic Party and the Republican Party. There are also several minor parties, called third parties. No member of a third party has won a presidential election since 1864, most times the public focus is on the two major parties, Republican and Democratic. Each party hosts a number of candidates who go through a nomination process to determine the presidential nominee for that party.

Democratic Party (United States) Presidential Candidates, 2008
- Barack Obama, U.S. Senator from Illinois
- Hillary Clinton, U.S. Senator from New York
- John Edwards, former U.S. Senator from North Carolina
- Bill Richardson, Governor of New Mexico

- Dennis Kucinich, U.S. Representative from Ohio
- Joe Biden, U.S. Senator from Delaware
- Mike Gravel, former U.S. Senator from Alaska
- Christopher Dodd, U.S. Senator from Connecticut
- Tom Vilsack, Former Governor of Iowa.

Republican Party (United States) Presidential Candidates, 2008

- John McCain, U.S. Senator from Arizona
- Mike Huckabee, former Governor of Arkansas
- Mitt Romney, Former Governor of Massachusetts
- Ron Paul, U.S. Representative from Texas
- Fred Thompson, former U.S. Senator from Tennessee
- Duncan Hunter, U.S. Representative from California
- Rudy Giuliani, Former Mayor of New York City
- Alan Keyes, former U.S. Ambassador from Maryland
- Sam Brownback, U.S. Senator from Kansas
- Jim Gilmore, former Governor of Virginia
- Tom Tancredo, former U.S. Representative from Colorado
- Tommy Thompson, former Governor of Wisconsin

The early Primaries and Caucuses are considered the most critical of the nomination process. The states that hold early primaries and caucuses are Iowa, New Hampshire, Nevada and South Carolina.

Before the Democratic primaries had even begun, the dichotomy of change versus experience had already become a common theme in the presidential campaign, with Senator Hillary Clinton positioning herself as the candidate with experience and Obama embracing the idea that he is the candidate of change.

In his announcement, Obama used the phrase that "Washington must change" as the theme of his campaign. Hillary Clinton adapted her experience as her campaign theme.

On Super Tuesday, Obama won voters who thought that the ability to bring change was the most important. Pre-election polling found that voters considered Obama's inexperience less of a problem than McCain's association with President George W. Bush. Obama's campaign pointed out that with McCain, it would just be "more of the same".

McCain did not help his campaign by picking first-term Alaska governor Sarah Palin to be his running mate. Palin excited the conservative base of the Republican Party with her speech at the 2008 Republican National Convention. Many republicans were not too happy with McCain's candidacy. Media interviews suggested that Palin lacked knowledge on certain key issues and they cast doubt among many voters about her qualifications to be Vice President or President. There was also fear that because of her conservative views she would alienate independents and moderates, two groups that most felt that McCain would need to win the election.

Entering 2008 George W. Bush was very unpopular. Polls were showing his percent of support in the twenties and thirties. In March 2008 McCain was endorsed by Bush at the White house. McCain supported the War in Iraq. He tried to show that he had disagreed with President Bush on many other key issues. During the entire election campaign, Obama pointed out that McCain had claimed in an interview that he voted with Bush 90% of the time, this was supported by Congressional voting records.

January 5, 2007—Meeting with G.W. Bush.
Senator Obama met with President George W. Bush and members of Congress at the White House.

January 7, 2007—Democratic Senator Joe Biden of Delaware declares he is running, and will set up an exploratory committee later in the month.

January 11, 2007—Democratic Senator Christopher Dodd of Connecticut officially announces his candidacy.

January 15, 2007—Republican Representative Tom Tancredo of Colorado establishes an exploratory committee.

January 17, 2007—Democratic Senator Barack Obama announces that he is forming an exploratory committee.

January 20, 2007—Democratic Senator Hillary Rodham Clinton announces that she is forming an exploratory committee. Senator Sam Brownback of Kansas officially announces his candidacy for the 2008 Republican presidential nomination in a rally in his home state.

January 31, 2007—Democratic Senator Joe Biden of Delaware formally and officially becomes a candidate.

February 1, 2007—The Democratic National Committee's annual winter meeting convenes in Washington, D.C., featuring ten presidential candidates.

10 February 2007—Obama announced his candidacy for President. Obama made his announcement in front of the Old State Capital, in Springfield, Illinois. This is the same place where in 1858 Abraham Lincoln delivered his famous House Divided speech against slavery.

Obama admired Abraham Lincoln because of his faith, even when success seemed impossible.

After announcing his candidacy for President, Obama said: "I recognize there is a certain presumptuousness—a certain audacity—to this announcement. I know I haven't spent a lot of time learning the ways of Washington. But I've been here long enough to know that the ways of Washington must change."

His speeches of change and the revolutionary campaign that he ran got him the Democratic nomination. He had accomplished what most could never imagine, seeing an African American become presidential nominee of a major political party.

Through most of 2007, John Edwards and Al Gore were behind Clinton and Obama.

February 11, 2007—Meeting with young people at Iowa State University rally. Obama's campaign successfully used the internet, through Facebook, to communicate with and organize young people. Many attended the rally that same day.

Volunteers that were brought together through Facebook.

February 12, 2007—Senator Obama addressed his supporters at a town-hall meeting at the University of New Hampshire in Durham, New Hampshire. (pg.14)

February 18, 2007—Senator Obama greets crowds at the Clark County Government Center during a stop in Las Vegas.

February 21, 2007—The first presidential forum is held in Carson City. [Source #1]

February 23, 2007—Obama held a rally in downtown Austin, Texas. Obama was good speaking at rallies. Many opponents complained that his speeches lacked substance.

Former Democratic Governor Tom Vilsack of Iowa withdraws from the race citing money problems.

February 28, 2007—Republican John McCain of Arizona states that he will formally announce his candidacy in April.

March 4, 2007—Barack Obama and Hillary Clinton came to Selma to commemorate the civil rights movement and reenactment of the march across the Edmund Pettas Bridge, where civil rights activists were beaten by police during a march in 1965.

After this event, Bill Clinton became more supportive of his wife, Hillary.

March 17, 2007—Obama spoke to supporters at the Farmers public market building in Oklahoma City, Oklahoma.

March 18, 2007—Senator Obama spoke to a Denver crowd of supporters.

April 12, 2007—Barack Obama wins a straw poll held at a virtual town hall debate between the Democratic candidates on the subject of the Iraq War, with 27.87 percent of the vote. 4,882 votes are cast.

April 25—April 27—John McCain launches his presidential campaign with stops in New Hampshire, South Carolina, Iowa, and Arizona.

May 2007—Obama was in Philadelphia for a campaign event.

May 31, 2007—Senator Obama spoke to a crowd in Aberdeen, South Dakota.

June 3, 2007—Democratic Debate between Senator John Edwards of North Carolina, Senator Hillary Clinton of New York and Senator Barack

Obama of Illinois was held at Saint Anselm College.

CNN hosted the Democratic debates in New Hampshire.

June 27, 2007—Senator Obama and Senator Clinton talked on the plane en route to the unity rally in New Hampshire.

June 29, 2007—Democratic Debate at Howard University, conducted by Tavis Smiley. Some African Americans did not like Tavis Smiley's criticism of Obama. Smiley resigned from *The Tom Joyner Morning Show* after that debate.

3 July 2007—Obama gave a speech in Keokuk, Iowa on 3 July 2007. Afterwards, Obama talked with supporters.

4 July 2007

23 July 2007—CNN/You Tube Debate was held at the Citadel, Charleston, South Carolina.

August 7, 2007—MSNBC and the AFL-CIO hosted a Democratic debate over labor issues in Chicago, Illinois.

August 19, 2007—A Democratic debate is hosted by ABC in Des Moines, Iowa.

September 18, 2007—Obama attended a rally in Washington, D.C., D.C. Mayor Adrian Fenty was also present.

September 27, 2007—Obama attended a rally in Washington Square Park in New York

In September 2007, Obama gave a keynote speech and received an honorary Doctor of Laws degree at Howard University's 140th convocation.

Southeastern University's president, Dr. Charlene Drew Jarvis was present for the event.

October 2007—After several debates Clinton, Edwards and Obama were ahead of other major candidates

October 30, 2007—Debate was hosted by NBC News and MSNBC in Philadelphia, Pennsylvania.

November 15, 2007—CNN and the Nevada Democratic Party held the Nevada Democratic presidential debate at the University of Nevada, Las Vegas in Las Vegas, Nevada.

November 21, 2007—Democratic candidate Barack Obama announces that television producer and media mogul Oprah Winfrey, who previously endorsed Obama, will appear with him on the campaign trail.

1 December 2007—After the Iowa Brown and Black Forum in Des Moines. Cris Dodd was one of the early ones to drop out of the Democratic race and endorse Obama.

December 8, 2007—Various campaign buttons were for sale at a campaign rally where television talk show host Oprah Winfrey endorsed Obama in Des Moines, Iowa.

December 9, 2007—Obama addressed a campaign rally at the Verizon Wireless Arena in Manchester, New Hampshire. Oprah Winfrey was present and also addressed the rally in support of Obama.

Obama made an unscheduled stop for pizza in Fairfield Iowa.

December 13, 2007—*The Des Moines Register* and Iowa Public Television hosted a Democratic debate in Johnston, Iowa.

December 18, 2007—there was a Campaign bus trip in Iowa near Sioux City, Iowa.

In the beginning of 2008, Obama began passing Clinton in the polls for the first time in Iowa. Obama won the Iowa caucus, John Edwards came in second and Clinton third.

Iowa was a first test. The speech by Obama at the Jefferson Jackson Dinner helped him recruit thousands of volunteers. He won a state that was 95% White. His win in Iowa got a lot of attention, according to his campaign manager. After Iowa they began raising 1,000,000 a day and he began to pick up endorsements.

Barack Obama wanted to reform the nation's health care system. He had personal knowledge of the reason that reform was necessary. He knew there would be challenges trying to bring cost and services into balance with needs.

President Obama had to propose his first federal budget, with a very large national debt, lagging revenue and a $2 trillion annual health care bill that still left 45 million Americans uninsured and consumed one quarter of the federal budget. The U.S. infant mortality rates are higher, and longevity rates lower than the rest of the industrial world.

January 3, 2008—The Iowa Democratic caucus was won by Barack Obama, the Republican caucus was won by Mike Huckabee.

Christopher Dodd and Joe Biden dropped out of the Democratic race.

January 5, 2008—Hillary Clinton, Barack Obama, Bill Richardson and John Edwards were at a televised debate at St. Anselm College in Manchester, New Hampshire.

January 8, 2008—The New Hampshire Democratic primary was won by Hillary Clinton. The Republican primary was won by John McCain. *The New Republic* published an article relating to a selection of newsletters published under the name of Republican candidate Ron Paul. The article described the news letters as showing an obsession with conspiracies and sympathy for the right-wing militia movement, and deeply held bigotry.

Obama thanked campaign volunteers for their services in Manchester, New Hampshire at Jervett Street School after winning the Iowa Caucuses.

January 10, 2008—Obama appeared with Senator John Kerry of Massachusetts during a rally at the College of Charleston. Senator Kerry and Senator Kennedy both endorsed Obama and he still could not carry Massachusetts.

January 15, 2008—The Michigan Democratic primary was won by Hillary Clinton, though no delegates were awarded. Only Clinton, Dennis Kucinich, Christopher Dodd and Mike Gravel were on the ballot. The Michigan Republican primary was won by Mitt Romney. Hillary Clinton, John Edwards and Barack Obama appeared at a Democratic debate in Las Vegas, Nevada.

January 19, 2008—The Nevada Democratic caucus was won by Hillary Clinton. The Republican caucus was won by Mitt Romney. The South Carolina Republican primary was won by John McCain. Republican candidate Duncan Hunter ends his campaign.

January 21, 2008—Debate University of Texas. Also Martin Luther King Day Celebration, in South Carolina. Senator Obama, Senator Clinton and former Senator John Edwards all took part in the celebration. Later that day, a Democratic rally took place at Myrtle Beach.

The Congressional Black Caucus Political Education and Leadership Institute hosted a Democratic debate in South Carolina.

January 24, 2008—A Republican presidential debate was held at Florida Atlantic University in Boca Raton, Florida. Dennis Kucinich dropped out of the Democratic race.

January 25—February 5, 2008—The Hawaii Republican caucuses were won by John McCain.

January 26, 2008—Primary Day South Carolina—Elsie Martin a poll Manager, had planned to retire, but decided to do one more campaign. She told Obama "Never give up because I know you can win" The South Carolina Democratic primary was won by Barack Obama.

January 27, 2008—Caroline Kennedy endorsed Barack Obama.

January 28, 2008—Senator Ted Kennedy announced his endorsement of Senator Obama for President.

January 30, 2008—Rudy Giuliani withdrew from the Republican race and endorsed John McCain. John Edwards dropped out of the Democratic race in New Orleans, Louisiana. Mike Huckabee, Ron Paul, John McCain and Mitt Romney appeared at a Republican debate at the Ronald Reagan Presidential Library in Simi Valley, California.

January 31, 2008—First one-on-one debate between Hillary Clinton and Barack Obama was at the Kodak Theater, Hollywood, California.

February 2, 2008—The Maine Republican caucus was won by Mitt Romney. MTV and MySpace co-hosted a debate, which was attended by Democrats Barack Obama and Hillary Clinton and Republicans Mike Huckabee and Ron Paul.

February 3, 2008—On the UCLA Campus, Oprah Winfrey, Caroline Kennedy and Stevie Wonder were there to show support for Obama at a rally sponsored by Michelle Obama.

February 5, 2008—Super Tuesday—Obama gave his Election Day speech in Chicago.

After Super Tuesday, Obama won ten straight victories. The campaign then began to move into states like Ohio, where Clinton had the advantage. She also had support of the Governor in Ohio.

In Southern Ohio, some people were saying that Obama was a Muslim. Many tried to say it was Senator Clinton's people who started the rumors. She later denounced it.

The people of Obama's campaign were blind sided by the Rev. Wright issue; they had to decide what to do. Obama's Speech in Philadelphia was a real show of leadership according to his campaign manager.

February 5, 2008—Twenty-four states and American Samoa hold primaries as a part of Super Tuesday, 2008. Full results:

- The Alabama Democratic primary was won by Barack Obama. The Republican primary was won by Mike Huckabee.
- The Alaska Democratic caucus was won by Barack Obama. The Republican caucus was won by Mike Huckabee.
- The Arizona Democratic primary was won by Hillary Clinton. The Republican primary was won by John McCain.
- The Arkansas Democratic primary was won by Hillary Clinton. The Republican primary was won by Mike Huckabee. The Green primary was won by Cynthia McKinney.
- The California Democratic primary was won by Hillary Clinton. The Republican primary was won by John McCain. The Libertarian primary was won by Christine Smith. The American Independent (the California affiliate of the Constitution Party) primary

was won by Don J. Grundmann. The Green and Peace and Freedom primaries were won by Ralph Nader.

- The Colorado Democratic caucus was won by Barack Obama. The Republican caucus was won by Mitt Romney.
- The Connecticut Democratic primary was won by Barack Obama. The Republican primary was won by John McCain.
- The Idaho Democratic caucus was won by Barack Obama.
- The Illinois Democratic primary was won by Barack Obama. The Republican primary was won by John McCain. The Green primary was won by Cynthia McKinney.
- The Kansas Democratic caucus was won by Barack Obama.
- The Massachusetts Democratic primary was won by Hillary Clinton. The Republican primary was won by Mitt Romney.
- The Minnesota Democratic caucus was won by Barack Obama. The Republican caucuses was won by Mitt Romney.
- The Missouri Democratic primary was won by Barack Obama. The Republican primary was won by John McCain. The Libertarian primary was won by "uncommitted".
- The New Jersey Democratic primary was won by Hillary Clinton. The Republican primary was won by John McCain.
- The New Mexico Democratic caucus was won by Hillary Clinton.

- The New York Democratic primary was won by Hillary Clinton. The Republican primary was won by John McCain

February 10, 2008—Senator Obama had a debate with Senator Clinton at the Walstern Center on Campus of Cleveland University.

Hillary Clinton's campaign manager Patti Solis Doyle resigns but remains with the campaign as senior adviser. Maggie Williams was announced as her successor. The Maine Democratic caucus was won by Barack

February 12, 2008—Democratic primaries was won by Barack Obama. The District of Columbia, Maryland, and Virginia Republican primaries were won by John McCain.

February 17, 2008—Barack Obama and former candidate John Edwards met at Edward's home in North Carolina to discuss the possibility of Edwards endorsing Obama.

February 20, 2008—Emmitt Smith of the Dallas Cowboys attended Obama's Rally at Reunion Arena in Dallas, Texas.

February 21, 2008—There was a Debate at University of Texas in Austin, between Hillary Clinton and Barack Obama, at the recreational sport center.

The Democrats Abroad primary was officially announced as having been won by Barack Obama.

February 26, 2008—Senator Obama had a debate with New York Democrat Senator Hillary Clinton at the Western Center on the campus of Cleveland University.

Hillary Clinton and Barack Obama debate in Ohio. Former Democratic candidate Christopher Dodd endorses Obama.

March 2, 2008—Houston rally.

March 3, 2008—Obama was at a town hall meeting with Veterans in San Antonio, Texas.

Obama was the only major candidate that opposed the Iraq War from the beginning.

March 4, 2008—Date of Texas Primary. Hillary Clinton won the Texas primary, but Obama won the Texas Caucuses and 99 delegates, while Hillary Clinton had only 94. Obama and his wife held an outdoor party in San Antonio.

Obama won the nomination by winning the Montana Primary and securing enough pledges of support from Democratic super delegates.

The Ohio, Texas and Rhode Island Democratic primaries are won by Hillary Clinton. The Vermont primary and Texas caucuses are won by Barack Obama. John McCain wins the Ohio, Rhode Island, Vermont and Texas Republican primaries, passing the 1,191-delegate threshold and becoming the Republican presumptive nominee. Mike Huckabee withdraws from the Republican race.

March 15, 2008—Obama gave a speech in Plainsfield, Indiana.

March 18, 2008—Obama gave a speech on race in Philadelphia—Acknowledging the history of anger between Blacks and Whites.

March 26, 2008—Mike Gravel withdrew from the Democratic race and announced that he will seek the Libertarian Party's presidential nomination.

April 13, 2008—Hillary Clinton and Barack Obama appeared at "The Compassion Forum" at Messiah College in Grantham, Pennsylvania.

April 16, 2008—Hillary Clinton and Barack Obama appeared at a debate at the National Constitution Center in Philadelphia, Pennsylvania.

April 21, 2008—Senator Obama's Campaign stopped at Pennsylvania State University's Allegheny Campus. Senator Obama spoke to supporters.

April 22, 2008—Pennsylvania Democratic primary was won by Hillary Clinton. Her win raised doubts about Obama's ability to connect with white working-class voters.

The Pennsylvania Democratic primary was won by Hillary Clinton. The Republican primary was won by John McCain.

May 3, 2008—Barack Obama won the Guam Democratic territorial convention by seven votes.

May 6, 2008—Hillary Clinton won the Indiana Democratic primary. The North Carolina Democratic primary was won by Barack Obama.

May 7, 2008—The North Carolina and Indiana Republican primaries were won by John McCain.

May 12, 2008—Obama held a rally at the Kentucky International Convention Center in Louisville. Obama did not do well with working-class white voters. Exit polls showed Hillary Clinton winning most of those voters. Obama was also having problems in Ohio, Pennsylvania and West Virginia. Most Democrats felt that he did not campaign aggressively enough in those states.

May 13, 2008—The West Virginia Democratic primary was won by Hillary Clinton. The Republican primary was won by John McCain. The Nebraska Republican primary was also won by John McCain.

May 14, 2008—Former Democratic candidate and 2004 vice presidential nominee John Edwards endorses Barack Obama.

May 18, 2008—Portland Oregon

May 19, 2008—The cover of *Time* Magazine feature a portrait of Obama.

May 20, 2008—Rally in Des Moines, Iowa.

The Oregon Democratic primary is won by Barack Obama. The Kentucky primary is won by Hillary Clinton. The Oregon and Kentucky Republican primaries are won by John McCain.

May 21, 2008—In the city of Obama in Japan

May 23, 2008—Campaign rally at the Bank Atlantic Center in Sunrise, Florida. A very large turn-out to hear Obama speak.

May 25, 2008—Obama delivers commencement address at Wesleyan University in Middletown,

Connecticut. He filled in for Senator Edward Kennedy, who was diagnosed as having a brain tumor.

May 31, 2008—The Democratic Party Leaders agreed to seat the disputes. Michigan and Florida delegates with half-votes at the summer convention.

Spoke in Aberdeen, South Dakota. Town hall meeting. The meeting was at The Civic Arena.

Senator Obama and his wife announced they had left Trinity United Church of Christ in Chicago. Resigning from Trinity was a difficult decision for the Obama's. (Reverend Wright)

June 1, 2008—The Puerto Rico Democratic primary is won by Hillary Clinton.

June 3, 2008—The final Democratic primary held in Montana and won by Obama. With the race over on June 5, 2008, Hillary Clinton officially concedes and ends her presidential bid. Barack Obama becomes the presumptive nominee for the Democratic Party.

Debate Hillary Clinton of New York and John Edwards of North Carolina and Senator Barack Obama of Illinois at St Anselm College.

The Montana primary is won by Barack Obama who also wins enough delegates to get the Democratic nomination.

June 4, 2008—Public Affairs Committee (AIPAC) policy—Washington Convention Center

June 5, 2008—Two days after securing the democratic nomination Obama knew that

Virginia was very important to his campaign. Bristow, Virginia—Obama launched his general election campaign two days after getting his party's nomination. He won the Virginia Primary.

Barack Obama appoints his vice presidential selection committee.

June 7, 2008—Hillary Clinton officially concedes the Democratic nomination and endorses Barack Obama.

June 15, 2008—Father's Day speech at Apostolic Church of God in Chicago. The speech was about fathers being involved in the raising of their children. The speech generated negative comments from some African Americans who were also Obama's supporters.

Technically, the nomination process for major political parties continues through June of the election year. Candidates were chosen by the end of the March primaries. However Barack Obama did not win enough delegates to get the nomination until June 3, 2008. After a long campaign against Hillary Clinton and the way Democratic state delegates contest were decided, the contest for nomination continued into June 2008.

June 16, 2008—Former Vice President Al Gore endorsed Obama at a rally at Joe Louis Arena in Detroit. Gore was the last big name Democrat to endorse Obama. Gore stayed neutral during the Democratic campaign. Most people thought he might endorse Clinton, because of their past relationship.

In June after all of the primaries were done, Barack Obama received the Democratic nomination for President. He was the first African American to win the nomination of a major political party.

June 17, 2008—Michelle Obama attends a fund raiser for her husband at designer Calvin Klein's home in New York.

June 27, 2008—Hillary Clinton joins Barack Obama at a rally in Unity, New Hampshire. This is her first public appearance since ending her presidential campaign.

July 19, 2008—Senator Barack Obama begins his tour of the Middle East and Europe with his first stop in Afghanistan. Obama meets with U.S. Military officials and heads of state in the countries he visits, which are Kuwait, Iraq, Jordan, Israel, Germany, France and Britain.

August 23, 2008—Senator Barack Obama announces that Senator Joe Biden from Delaware, and Chairman of the Senator Foreign Relations Committee, as his running mate.

August 25-28, 2008—The Democratic National Convention was held in Denver, Colorado.

August 27, 2008—Barack Obama is officially nominated for President by the Democratic Party. Joe Biden is nominated for Vice President of the United States.

Biden addressed the Democratic National Convention in Denver.

At the Democratic Convention at the Pepsi Center in Denver, Colorado, Obama was nominated, after Hillary Clinton called for Obama to be nominated by acclamation.

August 28, 2008—Barack Obama accepts the Democratic Party presidential nomination in a speech at Invesco Field in Denver, Colorado.

September 1-4, 2008—The Republican National Convention was held in Minneapolis, St. Paul Minnesota. John McCain is officially nominated for president and Sarah Palin is officially nominated for Vice President by the Republican Party. John McCain accepted the nomination in a speech at X Energy Center in St. Paul, Minnesota.

September 14, 2008—Senator John McCain announced Alaska Governor Sarah Palin as his running mate.

September 24, 2008—John McCain suspended his campaign to work on the financial crisis, and stated that he might not attend the first presidential debate on 26 September 2008. The first segment of Sarah Palin's interviews with Katie Couric aired.

September 26, 2008—The first presidential debate took place at the University of Mississippi, with a focus on foreign policy, national security and the economy, Jim Leirhner

October 2, 2008—

Joe Biden and Sarah Palin appeared at the vice presidential debate at Washington University in St. Louis. Gwen Ifill of PBS was moderator.

October 7, 2008—The second presidential debate took place at Belmont University in Nashville, Tennessee with a town hall format.

Sarah Palin accused Barack Obama of "palling around with terrorists" in reference to his alleged links with anti-war activist Bill Ayers. John McCain and Barack Obama appeared at the second presidential debate at Belmont University, Tennessee.

October 15, 2008—The last presidential debate took place at Hofstra University in Hemstead, New York with a domestic policy focus.

October 16, 2008—Barack Obama and John McCain address the traditional Alfred E. Smith Memorial Foundation Dinner.

October 19, 2008—Retired General and former Secretary of State under President George W. Bush, Colin Powell endorsed Barack Obama for President.

October 22, 2008—Senator Obama spoke at a campaign rally in Richmond, Virginia.

October 26, 2008—Constitution Party nominee Chuck Baldwin, Green Party nominee Cynthia McKinney and independent candidate Ralph Nader appeared at a debate at Columbia University, New York. It was covered by C-SPAN.

October 28, 2008—Presidential candidate Senator Barack Obama of Illinois and Senator Hillary Clinton of New York appeared at a rally together in Orlando, Florida.

October 29, 2008—The Obama campaign airs a 30-minute prime-time television ad on several networks, including a live component at the end of the broadcast.

Senator Obama spoke at a campaign rally at Osceola Heritage Park in Orlando, Florida.

October 30, 2008—Debate hosted by NBC News and MSNBC in Philadelphia Pennsylvania.

November 4, 2008—Obama won the national election, and became the forty fourth President of the United States of America and the first African American to do so.

Debates

September 26, 2008—Four debates were announced by the commission on Presidential Debates:

The first debate was at the University of Mississippi. The topic was supposed to be foreign policy and national security but because of the economic problems, there were questions on that topic. The moderator was Jim Lehrer of PBS.

October 2, 2008: the Vice Presidential debate was at Washington University in St. Louis.

The moderator was Gwen Ifill of PBS.

October 7, 2008: The second presidential debate was at Belmont University. The moderator of this debate was Tom Brokow of NBC. He addressed questions from the audience.

October 15, 2008—The third and final presidential debate was hosted at Hopstra University. It focused on domestic and economic policy. It had several segments with Bob Shieffer introducing the topics.

Throughout the campaign Obama went through Red and Blue states. Running what even his opponents described as a near flawless campaign. It was an Internet powered grassroots movement that virtually willed a voter base by asking people to donate as little as five dollars, asking them to recruit a friend to do the same. Providing them with e-mail updates on Obama's every move and directing them to the nearest polls by zip code on November 4. The campaign built its own voter bloc and became victory, through momentum and word of mouth. The candidate was not just a Black candidate with Black support, as television portrayed him to be.

During the Democratic Primaries, it was said he might not do well in some states because Black people only account for about 13 percent of the total U.S. population. Some in the press forgot that he won the Iowa caucuses over the front runner and most famous woman in politics, Hillary Clinton and over the former vice presidential candidate John Edwards, both of whom had deeply loyal fan bases in a state that was close to 95 percent White.

What made Obama distinctive was not his race but the machine-like discipline of an Ivy League professional over achiever, who seemed able to tap into the frustrations of an electorate, a country that was fed up with an exceptionally unpopular incumbent and looking for something to believe in.

Obama appealed to young people of all races and gender. He gave them someone and something to believe in.

He convinced people that he was not unpatriotic, being against the war in Iraq, but because he thought it was stupid.

Obama believed there was a need for health care reform. There were too many Americans that were uninsured. There were also people who were denied care because of insurance companies saying that some individuals had preexisting conditions that were not covered by the insurance that they had. Obama had personal information as to why there is a need for health care reform. He also had a personal experience that enhanced his desire to work hard on Health Care Reform. His mother had died at age 52. She had worked as a consultant, and could only purchase insurance when she got a new contract. Obama's mother became ill and after getting a new contract, she had to try and prove to the insurance company, that her illness was not a preexisting condition that she knew about. Obama wanted to make sure that insurance companies would no longer be able to discriminate against people who are sick.

Obama was also able to observe his grandmother continue to live in her home, and maintain her independence. This cost much less, than if she had gone into a long-term care facility. Based on the information Obama learned from his mother and grandmother's situation, convinced him that reforming health care was a top priority.

After being elected, he was able to get a Health Care bill passed.

Health Care Reform

The main things the new Law will do:

* Help millions of uninsured Americans get insurance.
* Pre-existing medical condition is no longer something insurers can use to deny coverage.
* Guarantee basic benefits to all Medicare recipients, and gradually close the "doughnut hole" in the Part D drug program.
* Begin a temporary program to help people with preexisting health conditions.
* Medical decisions will be between the patient and their doctor.
* Provide some new benefits for some people who already have insurance.
* Require most people to have coverage by 2014. Will offer help to people with low income and make more people eligible for Medicaid.
* Create state-run Insurance exchanges in 2014 that offer private insurance plans for uninsured and self-employed and people between jobs.
* Offer tax credits to small businesses to help them buy insurance for employees.
* It will keep Medicare financially sound for nearly 10 more years and reduce the deficit by an estimated $143 billion.

Some of the Campaign promises Obama made have already come to pass. His administration has approved a stimulus package to assist some states in providing employment for some citizens.

President Obama's administration has also changed the way credit card companies can charge fees, and to provide customers with more information about their agreements.

One of the hopes that Obama had if elected was to end the conflict in Iraq. Well during the week of August 18, 2010, there was an historical end to the 7 year war. The final U.S. Combat brigade left the country in a convoy to Kuwait. The Obama administration had promised to end the U.S. Combat mission by the end of August 2010. About 50,000 U.S. Troops will remain in Iraq, as a training force.

This was truly a historic military accomplishment. U.S. Commanders acknowledge that there are still some unresolved problems in Iraq that could threaten the security in the country.

By the end of August 2010, the U.S. will have the smallest number of troops in Iraq since the invasion in 2003. Those that remain are advisers and assess brigades, along with special operations forces. Their purpose will be to train Iraqi troops. Under a bilateral agreement, all U.S. troops must be out of Iraq by December 31, 2011.

More than 4,400 U.S. Service members have died in the Iraqi war. Many of these soldiers have served more than one tour; some as many as four.

These troops saw the end of a dictator and the rise of a powerful insurgency. The conflict lasted long after President George W. Bush declared the end of major combat operations in Iraq aboard an aircraft carrier May 1, 2003. The U.S. troops were thrust into the front lines of a brutal sectarian war that went on for over seven years. The troops helped secure elections that resulted in a government system more akin to an oligarchy than a parliamentary democracy.

It is clear that the departing troops are not leaving behind a peaceful country. That is why most troops drove out rather than flying out, that allowed the military to keep its last combat force a few weeks longer, so commanders can evaluate the risks of political instability.

Democrats did not get very much credit for the stimulus package. The country was going through a bad recession. The Congress was able to pass a bill that provided nearly 1 trillion dollars in spending and tax cuts. This money was supposed to help businesses with investments, keep local and state governments operating and put people to work.

Many people and some economists agree that the nationwide stimulus did some good. The administration stated that the stimulus may have saved or created over 3 million jobs, but the jobless rate continued to rise.

It is believed that the recession was far worse than predicted. Some republicans campaigning for Congress stated that President Obama's economic policies had failed.

Senate passes health-care bill on 60-39 vote. Senate Democrats approved legislation on Christmas Eve that would change the health-care system by requiring people without insurance to get coverage. The bill will protect those who have insurance from private insurance practices.

This was probably the most important vote that these members of the Senate will make during their tenure. The Senate and the House then had to try to blend their different approaches to providing coverage and paying for it. The Republicans vowed to make the process as difficult as possible. They hoped to stop the legislation.

Other Presidents have tried and failed to pass comprehensive health insurance reform.

President Obama said that once the House and Senate merge their bills, this will be the most important piece of social legislation since the Social Security Act passed in the 1930s and the most important reform of our health-care system since Medicare passed in the 1960s.

The Senate bill passed without one vote from Republicans.

There was a continued debate for almost a year.

The Republicans had support from the insurance lobbying group American Health Insurance Plans. Most major business groups saw reform as a threat to jobs and health coverage that people receive through their employers.

The White House made deals with drug companies and hospital groups: AARP and the American Medical Associations, endorsed both the House and Senate bills.

The Majority Leader and the House Speaker had to make concessions on major issues. Both bills include restrictions on abortion coverage. Many of the stipulations infuriated liberals but were necessary to win over conservative Democrats.

On April 23, 2010, President Obama went to New York to deliver a stern address to financial executives. He was telling them that greater government oversight was in the best interest of the country and the industry. This speech was the culmination of a month long involvement of President Obama with the issue of financial reform.

After that meeting with people on Wall Street, the President turned his attention to political leaders. He said: "We've seen misleading arguments and attacks that are designed not to improve the bill but to weaken or to kill it. We've seen a bipartisan process buckle under the weight of these withering forces, even as we've produced a proposal that by all accounts is a commonsense, reasonable, non-ideological approach to target the root problems that lead the turmoil in our financial sector and ultimately in our entire economy."

There were over 700 members in the audience from both the financial and political sectors.

White House officials had said the president was there to prod Wall Street to cooperate, not to lecture.

President Obama's focus on financial regulations comes after Treasury Secretary Timothy F Geithner and a team of administration aides spent over a year on the ground work, while others in the White House were involved in the fight over health-care legislation. After the Health Care Bill was signed, the President's role seem to consist of two parts, making the public case that financial reform was necessary, and privately lobbying lawmakers to pass a bill. President Obama used his radio and internet address to criticize Republican opposition, and threatened to veto legislation that did not meet his goals.

During a CNBC interview, he discussed in detail the complex issue of regulatory derivatives.

The remarks that the President made about the connection between Wall Street and ordinary citizens was related to a speech he gave two years earlier: "I believe in a strong financial sector that helps people to raise capital and get loans and invest their savings. That's part of what has made America what it is," he said.

> "But a free market was never meant to be a free license to take whatever you can get, however you can get it," he said. "That's what happened too often in the years leading up to this crisis. Some—and let me be

clear, not all—on Wall Street forgot that behind every dollar traded or leveraged, there is a family looking to buy a house, pay for an education, open a business, save for retirement. What happens on Wall Street has real consequences across our country, across our economy."

In January of 2010, things were not going very well for Democrats. First there was the election of Scott Brown to fill the seat in the Senate of Senator Edward Kennedy. Scott Brown was a Massachusetts state senator, who won by running against the health-care legislation that Senator Kennedy was for, prior to his death. Senator Kennedy was one of President Obama's strongest supporters. This was a surprise upset, because Senator Kennedy had held his senate seat for 47 years.

Most people thought that Martha Coakley, the Democratic candidate would have an easy win. Some Democrats did not think that she campaigned very hard. Coakley's campaign said that the Democratic organization did not provide enough help with fund raising. The Democratic organization stated they received Coakley's Campaign's call for help too late. The help they provided was not enough to turn the situation around. President Obama went to Boston on the Sunday before the election to try to rally voters for Coakley. It appeared that it was too late for the Presidents visit to be helpful. It seems that Brown ran a better campaign. It also appeared that Brown's opposition to the health-care legislation was the main reason for his success.

There seems to be a lot of people who don't agree with the health-care legislation. Democrats will have to do a better job of pointing out the benefits of the health-care legislation, to negate the negative comments being made by Republicans.

In January 2010, a 20 year old man from Bethesda, Maryland was sentenced to 61 months in prison for his involvement in a plot to try to kill President Obama.

The young man's name is Colin McKenzie-Gude. The judge technically sentenced McKenzie-Gude on his earlier guilty plea of storing bomb-making chemicals in his bedroom. Because of some other factors, prosecutors were able to convince Judge Messitte that McKenzie-Gude deserved additional prison time because he was plotting to kill Mr. Obama during the 2008 presidential campaign. He had also made an attack plan against another student who was possibly going to sell him untraceable guns and he had not accepted responsibility for his actions. The judge also criticized McKenzie-Gude's parents for giving their only child too much lee-way, inside his second-floor bedroom in their house. McKenzie-Gude stored the chemicals, three semi-automatic rifles, two shotguns and hundreds of rounds of ammunition, including armor-piercing rounds. Police also found assault plans on a computer storage device in the bedroom.

The judge made it clear that he wanted to deter others. "There are other Colin McKenzie-Gudes out there who are perhaps 10, 12, 13, 14," Judge Messitte said. "And they're fascinated with explosives, and they're going to watch this case and know about this case." Judge Messitte was also clearly concerned that a former friend of McKenzie-Gude, Patrick Yevsukov, testified that McKenzie-Gude had talked about trying to assassinate Obama by halting his convoy with roadside bombs. The judge said it "seemed to be a serious plan."

Judge Messitte said McKenzie-Gude is a product of a part of society that seems to think it is all right to engage in role-playing when it comes to talk of using weapons.

"You can talk a game of creating havoc, and then you perhaps think you can come to court afterwards and say, 'I didn't really mean that. I was all play-acting, I think I'd like to be home with my parents now,'" Judge Messitte said. "The real world does not operate that way. And it never should. And you need to know that." Collin McKenzie Gude was sentenced to five years for his action.

President Obama outlined his first-year legislative record, which he said had rescued the economy and put it on a long term growth path. There were some things that he thought might be more difficult to achieve.

There were those who believed that President Obama had compromised too much to secure health-care reform. Some people felt he gave too much authority to congressional leaders in his pursuit of his legislative agenda. President Obama had some signature initiatives, such as cap—and trade legislation and financial regulatory reform. President Obama defended his legislative record at a time when his approval ratings were the lowest of his presidency. As the Senate prepares to pass its version of health-care reform legislation, it would appear that President Obama's administration has had a very successful year.

On Tuesday 22 December 2009, Democrats began celebrating the imminent approval by Senate of an overhaul of the nation's health-care system. Senator Max Baucus (D-Mont.), stated that the 'finish line is in sight," he was the chief planner of the bill. He made his statement shortly after the Senate voted 60 to 39, to advance the $871 billion health package. Senator Baucus stated, "We're not the first to attempt such reforms. We will be the first to succeed."

No two career beginnings are ever the same, but Obama's beginning is very much like several other Democrats—Franklin D. Roosevelt, John F. Kennedy, Jimmy Carter and Bill Clinton.

It was stated by many people after Obama's election, that Robert F. Kennedy predicted in 1968 that the United States would elect a black president in 40 years. Mr. Obama's election was less than forty years.

In June 2010, the war in Afghanistan was not going well. There were combat delays, increased casualties and reports of Afghan corruption. There was also talk about the possibility of General Stanley McChrystal being fired. General McChrystal had made disrespectful comments about President Obama's policy team.

Gen. McChrystal's critical remarks of some of President Obama's administration's top officials did not leave the president much of a choice.

The comments made by the general were insubordination and could not just be overlooked by the president. He had to make a difficult choice even though the war in Afghanistan was not going very well. The remarks were made by Gen. McChrystal and members of his inner circle, in an article in *Rolling Stone* magazine. General McChrystal had made an informal offer to senior military officials to resign before going back to Washington, but President Obama had made it clear that he would determine the general's fate. Most military and political officials felt that McChrystal had crossed the line of respect, in criticizing his civilian chain of command. Defense Secretary Robert M. Gates said McChrystal made a "significant mistake" and used "poor judgment".

Many military personnel felt that the president had no choice except to fire the general.

General McChrystal flew to Washington to explain why he and his aides had made the remarks in the *Rolling Stone* magazine: calling the national security adviser a "clown", described Obama as intimidated and disengaged, disparaging allies and top U.S. diplomats, and converting Vice President Biden's surname to Bite Me. Anyone reading the article will agree that it is without a doubt insubordination.

President Obama fired General Stanley A. McChrystal on Wednesday 23 June 2010. The president concluded that the general had damaged the chain of Command and could no longer work effectively with the civilian leadership at a critical moment in the War. The president knew the importance of preserving the authority of the Commander in Chief. Appointing General David H. Petraeus to the Afghan Command allowed the president to keep his war strategy intact.

President Obama's firing of General McChrystal, removed any fear of the president appearing weak. It was believed that Gen. Petraeus's appointment would have Senate confirmation quickly.

The firing of Gen. McChrystal ended his 34-year Army career.

For many weeks Mrs. Obama had been telling her friends and her staff that she was not happy with her present role. She wanted to be involved in things that would allow her to utilize her qualifications. She has qualifications in public policy, law and management.

She wanted to do more, so she changed her chief of staff. The new chief of staff is a close friend, Susan Sher. Mrs. Obama felt that her new chief of staff would get her and her team more involved in the West Wing's activities. She wanted to be a part of child nutrition reauthorization act, prevention and wellness for health-care reform.

Mrs. Obama will soon talk about the creation of an advisory board to help military families. She will also be the point person for the national services programs, United We Serve, which she launched this month.

On Tuesday 22 June 2010 President Obama met with many executives of major insurance companies at the White House. The president wanted to caution them against using requirements in the new health-care reform legislation as a reason to raise premiums.

"There are genuine cost drivers that are not caused by insurance companies. But what is also true is that we've got to make sure this new law is not being used as an excuse to simply drive up costs," the president said in a brief speech afterward. "The CEOs here today need to know that they're going to be required to justify unreasonable premium increases."

Karen Ignagni, president of the trade association America's Health Insurance Plans, said she and other industry representatives found the meeting to be a "very constructive" opportunity to make the case that the main cause of rising premiums is not industry greed but recessionary pressures and increasing medical and drug costs.

"For instance, in the small employer and individual market, the economy is causing younger, healthier people to drop coverage, which means that the costs of the [remaining] risk pool is higher because it's older and sicker," she said.

The president's speech mark the first 90 days since the president signed the measure into law. It also provided the president an opportunity to mention the consumer protections in the legislation that take effect in the year 2010. These include bans on several discriminatory insurance practices for which specific regulations were issued Tuesday 22 June 2010. As of September 23, 2010, no plan will be allowed to revoke coverage of sick members who make unintentional mistakes on their applications or to set lifetime limits on coverage. The administration estimated that more than 100 million Americans face such limits. Most plans will be barred from excluding children with preexisting conditions. Existing plans purchased by individuals—as opposed to employers—will be exempt from that protection. But it will be extended to all Americans by 2014.

The new rules also phase out most health plans' ability to impose annual dollar limits on benefits.

Initially, employer plans issued or renewed beginning September 23, 2010, as well as new individual plans, will have to set annual limits no lower than $750,000. That minimum will be raised to $1.25 million the following year, and to $2 million the year after that. Plans issued or renewed after January 1, 2014, will be prohibited from setting any annual limits on benefits the administration deems "essential".

Employers and insurers that wish to delay complying with the new annual limits can apply for an exemption. But they will have to prove to federal authorities that raising their annual limits would force them to significantly reduce coverage or increase rates.

All new plans will have to allow parents to designate any available participating pediatrician as their children's primary-care doctor, permit women to see OB-GYNs without a referral from a primary care doctor and charge the same for emergency services obtained out of the plan's network of hospitals as those provided in network.

The most broad and controversial elements of the new law will not take effect until 2014. That include a requirement that all Americans obtain insurance and the creation of a state based "exchanges" through which people who are not covered by their employer can buy plans at competitive rates.

On Tuesday 31 August, 2010, President Obama declared the U.S. War in Iraq over. He was letting the country know that he was making good on one of his campaign pledges. "Tonight, I am announcing that the American combat mission in Iraq has ended," President Obama said in his second prime-time address from the Oval Office. He spoke again of his belief "that out of the ashes of war, a new beginning could be born in this cradle of civilization." In his speech, the president sought to unshackle the nation from a military invasion, begun by his predecessor that was supposed to swiftly depose a dictator, seize hidden weapons of mass destruction and leave behind a democratic government. Instead the war went on for over seven years with American troops against an expanding insurgency. The war became a recruiting element and training ground for al-Qaeda and other terrorist groups. The president noted the "huge price" the United States paid during the conflict. During the course of the war 1.5 million troops served in Iraq, many had multiple tours. Over 4,400 died, and 32,000 were wounded.

After his remarks on withdrawing combat troops from Iraq, the president noted his other priorities. He said resources could now shift to the war in Afghanistan and to boosting the economy, which he said was "our most urgent task."

It was said that before his speech, President Obama called former president George W. Bush.

The speech came at a time set by President Obama for combat troops to leave Iraq. The departure is not related to any progress on the ground in Iraq, and the government has not yet been formed. Though combat troops have left Iraq, 50,000 troops remain as advisers and may still suffer some casualties. The president believed that the US could apply the resources needed to improve the situation in Afghanistan. The president linked the ending of the war to the U.S. economy, his most pressing problem two months before midterm elections. "Today, our most urgent task is to restore our economy and put the millions of Americans who have lost their jobs back to work. To strengthen our middle class, we must give all our children the education they deserve, and all our workers the skills that they need to compete in a global economy," President Obama said. "We must jump-start industries that create jobs, and end our dependence on foreign oil. We must unleash the innovation that allows new products to roll off our assembly lines, and nurture the ideas that spring from our entrepreneurs. This will be difficult but in the days to come, it must be our central mission as a people, and my central responsibility as president."

President Obama in reference to Father's Day brought together children, famous dads and nonprofit groups that promote fatherhood to highlight the importance of fathers.

The celebration was at the ARC, the arts and recreation campus in Southeast Washington.

The president was there to announce the creation of the President's Fatherhood and Mentoring Initiative. It will build on a theme that has been central to the president's family policy and a core part of the White House's Office of Faith-based and Neighborhood Partnerships.

The new initiative will expand on a six-city listening tour the administration held last year to bring attention to the issue of fatherlessness.

Roland Warren, president of the National Fatherhood Initiative, which was founded in 1994 and recently contracted with the federal government to produce public service announcements promoting fatherhood.

On Tuesday, August 10, 2010, President Obama approved and signed into law a $26 billion plan. This was in an effort to assist the economic recovery. The plan was to save the jobs of thousand of teachers and other government workers. This will make the total direct federal spending on the economy approximately $1.2 trillion since the recession began in late 2007.

The economic growth has been slow and unemployment stuck at 9.5 percent. Senior Democrats and officials of the administration stated that the state aid package would probably be the last effort of economic stimulus until after the congressional elections in November.

Democrats believed that the package would save the jobs of 300,000 workers by helping state governors with their budget problems.

Most Republican argued that the plan would not help the economy any more than the stimulus package president Obama signed after taking office in January 2009.

The total of the bill was much less than what Mr. Obama had requested. Democratic leaders had to be sure the cost of the package would not increase future deficits. President Obama also approved several extensions of unemployment benefits.

President Obama on Monday August 30, 2010, said that he and his economic team were discussing "additional measures" to bolster growth and spur hiring, including "further tax cuts" to encourage businesses to create jobs. The president said he would provide details "in the days and weeks to come." Meanwhile, he urged Senate Republicans to drop their "blockade" of a Democratic measure aimed at aiding small businesses by cutting their taxes and creating a $30 billion loan fund to give them easier access to credit.

President Obama spoke of other policy initiatives in the works, including plans to extend Bush administration tax cuts for the middle class that are set to expire in January. The president's economic policy also has plans to increase investments in clean energy and corporate research, rebuild the nation's physical and communications infrastructure; and provide tax cuts to encourage small businesses to hire new workers.

The revolutionary ideas continue. The Obama administration is a supporter of allowing federal employees to work from home. The head of the General Services Administration was sworn in over the telephone. She was unable to get into Washington because of a snowstorm. Martha Johnson put one hand on the Bible, raised the other hand while her husband held the phone to her mouth, and she was sworn in. The large snowstorms inspired President Obama to issue orders to the director of the Office of Personnel Management. "The president made it clear to the director that he doesn't want snow, nature, or any other cause to be able to stop our government." OPM had no control over the weather or plows, telework is the only way to achieve the goal that the president had set.

The wider use and acceptance of telework is becoming a reality. Last month in September 2010, the Senate unanimously passed telework legislation and the House could do so during the lame-duck session. The bill would require federal agencies to appoint telework managers and incorporate the option into contingency operations. Once it's passed, OPM director and other authorities plan to make the option automatic for all federal employees who could do their jobs away from the office. OPM Director Berry said, "It will boost morale, I would argue, it decreases distractions and it reduces time and the environmental impact of commuting." "In example after example, it leads to happier, more productive employees. Newer workers want to take a laptop or iPad home or to a café."

Younger workers also want almost constant feedback from supervisors, "and they're happy to get that online," Berry said. GSA is already working to determine which workers are eligible and ready to telework.

On May 10, 2010 President Barack Obama announced his selection of Elena Kagan for Associate Justice of the Supreme Court of the United States, to replace retiring Justice John Paul Stevens. Kagan's nomination was confirmed by a 63-37 vote of the United States Senate on August 5, 2010.

Elena Kagan was Solicitor General of the United States, when she was nominated. She had been appointed as Solicitor General by Barack Obama. She was previously a contender for retiring David Souter's seat in 2009, but was passed over in favor of current Supreme Court Justice Sonia Sotomayer.

Kagan's nomination was received positively by most Democrats in the Senate. They complimented her abilities. Republicans were quick to criticize her handling of military recruiters during her time as Dean of Harvard Law School. The Deans of over one-third of the country's law schools, 69 total, endorsed Kagan's coalition—building skills and "understanding of both doctrine and policy" as well as her written record of legal analysis. On July 20, 2010, the Senate Judiciary Committee voted to endorse Kagan with only one Republican vote.

President Obama nominated Judge Sonia Sotomayor for the Supreme Court. She is the first Hispanic in history to be nominated to be a justice.

Judge Sotomayor was born to a Puerto Rican family. Her father died when she was nine years old. After her father's death Sotomayor turned to books for solace. She says it was her love of Nancy Drew books that led her to the law.

Judge Sotomayor graduated as valedictorian of her class at Blessed Sacrament and at Cardinal Spellman High School in New York. She won a scholarship to Princeton where she continued to excel, graduating summa cum laude and Phi Beta Kappa. She was a co-recipient of the M.Taylor Pyne Prize, the highest honor Princeton awards to an undergraduate. At Yale Law School, Judge Sotomayor served as editor of the Yale Law Journal and as managing editor of the Yale Studies in World Public Order.

After law school, Sotomayor spent five years as Assistant District Attorney in Manhattan, trying dozen of criminal cases. Robert Morgenthau, who chose her for the position, described her as a "fearless and effective prosecutor." She entered private practice in 1984, working as an "international corporate litigator handling cases involving everything from intellectual property to banking, real estate and contract law.

Tome Goldstein of SCOTUSBlog writes, "Almost all of her career has been in public service——as a prosecutor, trial judge. She has almost no money to her name," the White House notes.

Judge Sotomayor will bring more federal judicial experience to the Supreme Court than any justice in 100 years, and more overall judicial experience than anyone confirmed for the Court in the past 70 years.

Judge Sotomayor became the first Latina to serve on the U.S. Court of Appeals for the Second

Circuit, one of the most demanding circuits in the country. She has practiced in over 3000 panel decisions and authored roughly 400 opinions, handling difficult issues of constitutional law, to complex procedural matters, to lawsuits involving complicated business organizations.

According to notes and other information cited in a new book by journalist Bod Woodward, President Obama had looked for a way out of the war in Afghanistan during 2009. He was pressing his top military advisors for an exit plan that they never gave him. According to the book, the president was frustrated with his military commanders only offering options that required more troops, so the president finally crafted his own strategy, dictating a classified six-page "terms sheet" that sought to limit U.S. involvement.

According to Woodward's meeting—by-meeting, memo-by-memo account of the 2009 Afghan strategy review, the president avoided talk of victory as he described his objectives, "This needs to be a plan about how we're going to hand it off and get out of Afghanistan," Obama is quoted as telling White House aides as he laid out his reasons for adding 30,000 troops in a short-term escalation. "Everything we're doing has to be focused on how we're going to get to the point where we can reduce our footprint. It's in our national security interest. "There cannot be any wiggle room."

Obama rejected the military's request for 40,000 troops as part of an expansive mission that had no foreseeable end. "I'm not doing 10 years," he told Secretary of Defense Robert M. Gates and Secretary of State Hillary Rodham Clinton at a meeting on October 26, 2009. "I'm not doing long term nation-building. I am not spending a trillion dollars."

Woodward's book portrays Obama and the White House as barraged by warnings about the threat of terrorist attacks on U.S. soil and confronted with the difficulty in preventing them. During an interview with Woodward in July, the president said: "We can absorb a terrorist attack. We'll do everything we can to prevent it, but even a 9/11, even the biggest attack ever . . . we absorbed it and we are stronger."

Democrats were not able to get one Republican to begin debates on a defense authorization bill that included the repeal of the military's "don't ask, don't tell" policy. The policy bans gay men and women from serving openly in the armed forces.

Democrats were unable to repeal the law, even with White House backing and majorities in Congress.

The policy began under President Bill Clinton. Democrats thought this was the best time to try to repeal the policy after President Obama had support from Secretary Robert M. Gates and other military leaders.

Republicans objected that Majority Leader Harry. M. Reid had attached several politically motivated proposals to the measure. Senator John

McCain, a republican from Arizona, led the charge against the repeal.

Advocates of the repeal blamed the White House and Democrats in the Congress for not acting sooner.

White House officials and Senate Democratic leaders said they hoped to revive the issue after the November election.

There has been a lot of talk about President Obama may be just a one-term president. A lot is about what the president does over the last two years of his term. He must make it clear that his focus will be on the major problems that concern Americans. The economic problems and especially employment, so that people can meet their financial obligations.

During President Obama's campaign, he spoke of his desire to change the way Washington works. He can renew that desire by trying to create a government of national unity, and not campaigning for a second term. The president once said in an interview with Diane Sawyer, "I'd rather be a really good one-term president than a mediocre two-term president."

Being less political would give him greater leverage with some republicans, and make it harder for opponents, who are doing all they can to insure that President Obama is a one-term president.

At a meeting on Tuesday President Obama and congressional Republicans were determined to reach an agreement on the tax cuts that were due to expire at the end of 2010. There was a possibility of a compromise that would avoid a tax increase for all American workers.

There was no formal agreement made at this meeting, but most attending thought the meeting was positive. The participants believed they could get an agreement that would result in a temporary extension of all the tax cuts, and the ratification of a nuclear arms treaty with Russia, the continuation of unemployment benefits and funding for government operations into next year. There were many who doubted that Congress's lame duck session would produce any positive legislation.

One of the accomplishments of the meeting was the formation of a bipartisan group to seek a solution to the disagreement over taxes. The group—Treasury Secretary, Timothy F. Geithner, White House budget director, Jacob Lew and two lawmakers from each party.

"We should work to make sure that taxes will not go up by thousands of dollars on hard-working middle-class Americans come January 1st, which would be disastrous for these families, but also could be crippling for the economy," President Obama told supporters. The group agreed that they should try to resolve the issues before the year end.

Republicans insisted that the tax cuts, enacted under President George W. Bush, be extended for all income groups. Most congressional Democrats are opposed to extending tax cuts for household income above $250,000. The President and his aides showed that they were willing to compromise on some points. President Obama said he hoped the meeting would serve simply as a "first step toward a new and productive working relationship" between the two parties.

In an effort to appeal to Republicans on deficits, President Obama proposed a two-year pay freeze for civilian federal workers.

The White House and congressional Republicans began working on a deal that would prevent taxes from going up on any American families. There was the problem of the tax cuts that expire at the end of December, renewing the unemployment benefits and keeping the government funded for next year.

Many of the democrats thought that President Obama was being too quick to accommodate the Republicans. The Republicans were demanding that Democrats extend Bush income tax cuts at all levels not just for the middle class. President Obama was seeking Republican support for 13 months of unemployment benefits and as tax cuts for working families. Failure to renew the benefits could do great harm to jobless families. Republicans resisted, saying that if jobless benefits are extended the cost should be covered by cutting spending some place else.

Midterm elections are not very happy times for the president and his party. The 2010 was especially difficult for President Obama and the Democrats.

There were three major priority topics, the economy, campaign finance laws and the tea party.

Almost anyone you talk with knows someone who has lost their job in the past year. Many are not sure if they can cover the next month's mortgage or rent payment, so many feel that no one in the government cares about their problems.

There also was a new movement called the tea party. It could be called one of the opposition's revolutionary battles. It disrupted the normal order of the Republican Party. There is also concern over the status of the tea party, is it just a temporary phase or a permanent movement.

One of the most closely watched races was between Majority Leader Harry M. Reid and Sharron Angle, a tea party republican. Senator Reid won, even though Republicans had hoped that they would be able to remove Sen. Reid from his position. The GOP did win control of the House and Democrats were able to keep control of the Senate. Republican candidates gained their edge because voters were concerned about the economy and the large number of independents that were unhappy with Obama's victory in 2008.

Voters gave their votes to republicans hoping it would send a message to the democrats that are presently in power. It could be said that they also sent a message to republicans by not changing control of the Senate. Voters were not hoping for a revolution, they were hoping for a Congress working together to solve some of the major problems the country has. It seems that neither party is truly in agreement with the needs and desires of most of the voters so the revolution continues.

The Republicans won enough seats during the midterm election to gain control of the Congress. The House and the Senate have such a difference of objectives that it may affect the way debates are decided during the next two years. Many of the House freshmen are new in politics and very ambitious. Many of them believe their main goal was to derail President Obama's agenda and scale back the size of the federal government.

The leader of the House is Rep. John A. Boehner (R-Ohio), who won as a benefit of the tea party. After Rep. Boehner accepted the speaker's gavel from Nancy Pelosi (D-Calif.) who is now the minority leader. After the formal roll-call vote for the gavel concluded, Boehner received 241 votes and Pelosi received 173 votes ending her four year term as the first female speaker of the House.

Speaker Pelosi in a final speech, congratulated Boehner. She said "I now pass this gavel and the sacred trust that goes with it to the new speaker, God bless you, Speaker Boehner," With a few tears, Boehner took the speaker's gavel. Many began to congratulate him, and shortly after Boehner disappeared for an hour and came back when he was officially made speaker.

The Senate, which is still controlled by Democrats, has the same leader, Harry M. Reid (D-Nev.) He narrowly won a fifth term in November. He was against a tea party opponent.

As he opened the new Senate, Sen. Reid, who is 70 years, asked his Republican colleagues to end what he called their obstructionist ways, setting the tone for coming battles over deficit reduction, the war in Afghanistan, heath-care reform and taxes.

"The most important change we can make in the 112th Congress is to work better and more closely as teammates, not as opponents—as partners, not as partisans—to fulfill our constitutional responsibility to pursue a more perfect union" Sen. Reid said.

Not many of the items on the House leader's agenda are likely to end up in law as conceived—beginning with the GOP effort to repeal President Obama's heath-care law.

The financial crisis began on Wall Street, where bets on risky mortgage loans resulted in enormous losses. More than 4 million jobs were lost in just six months. As work continues to repair our financial infrastructure to get the economy moving again, we need action to prevent or stall the next financial crisis.

Retiring baby boomers will live longer on average than previous generations. This will have a great impact on government spending. The National Commission on Fiscal Responsibility and Reform and the Bipartisan Policy Center have steps for addressing the problem. Both propose to reduce and cap discretionary spending, tax reform, reduce mandatory spending on health care and other programs, and ensure the long-term solvency of Social Security. Fixing these problems will require a national bipartisan commitment to a comprehensive group of spending and tax cuts over many years.

There is great optimism for economic growth in 2011. There are many things that can hinder growth, but there are also reasons for optimism such as government actions to boost growth are starting to take effect, a payroll tax cut beginning January 1, 2011, and a massive Federal Reserve action that was announced on November 3, 2010. Americans have also made progress paying down their consumer debts and saving more. The stock market has risen steadily in recent months; this will increase businesses' confidence. There was the smallest number of individuals filing for unemployment since the summer of 2008. The unemployment rate could increase even as the economy strengthens. If large numbers of Americans who had dropped out of the workforce came back into the workforce and it increased to pre-recession levels, many would not be able to find jobs right away. This would cause the rate to increase.

After passage of the President's Health Care bill, many republicans complained about it. Most were not suggesting changes to certain parts of the plan, but were saying the entire plan should be repealed.

The Republicans had one of the largest midterm elections victories in recent history. After being sworn into office, many of the new Republican leaders pledged to derail President Obama's agenda. One of the items at the top of Republican's list was to repeal the Democrats' health-care bill. This was a pledge that Republican candidates made during the midterm election campaigns. Republicans stated they would keep pushing to overturn the law. They said they would try to change it by eliminating certain parts of the law, such as a requirement that nearly all Americans obtain health insurance—and working to replace others. They also hoped to have Democratic support on a proposal to remove a tax on businesses, an idea President Obama has indicated he is willing to consider. Each side spoke of seeking a bipartisan way to take another look at certain parts of the law, to see if certain parts needed some changes. Democrats said they were willing to discuss possible changes to certain parts of the law. Democrats did not believe that Republicans could devise a better plan. After all they had control of Congress for 12 years and they had a Republican president for 6 years. If it was possible for them to produce a better plan, why not then?

The House finished business at noon Friday and would begin its first full week on Tuesday.

Rep. Gabrielle Giffords had just been sworn in for her third term in Congress. She planned to return to Tucson for the weekend and events she had planned.

Saturday just before 10 o'clock a.m., she drove from her home to the Safeway on North Oracle Road; just outside the Tucson city limits, in an area suburb, Casas Adobes.

There were those who needed help from their representative and some who just wanted to meet Congresswoman Giffords.

Christina Taylor Green, was born on September 11, 2001, came to learn more about her government. She was a third grader who had just been elected to student council.

Gabe Zimmerman, a social worker, who organized Giffords's forums. He was also engaged to be married.

Jared Lee Loughner took a cab to the Safeway, police said. The fare was $14, and the passenger had only a $20.00 bill and the cab driver did not have change. They walked into the supermarket to get change for the $20.00 bill.

Rep. Gabrielle Giffords wanted to create a sense of community and also change the negative image of government. She was concerned about a Sarah Palin's Web site which put Giffords's district in the cross hairs of a gunsight, this was during a previous campaign of Giffords's, where someone shot a pellet through the glass door of Rep. Giffords's Tucson office. Her Republican opponent invited supporters to a Saturday morning campaign event where they could shoot an M16 and "Get on Target for Victory in November."

Giffords's husband, Mark Kelly is an astronaut, based in Houston, getting ready for a shuttle launch in April.

Eyewitness accounts of the moments before, during and after the mass shooting that killed six people and injured 14 others, including Rep. Gabrielle Giffords, Democrat from Arizona were as follows:

On January 8, 2011 Rep. Giffords arrives at the Safeway at 10 a.m. She walks up to the table set up outside the entrance, said good morning to the constituents standing in line to see her. At 10:10 a.m. Giffords is talking to two people when a gunman approaches and fires several shots point blank. After Giffords falls, a number of people near her try to flee but are trapped, hemmed in by the table and a concrete post. Three people behind the table are dead, including Judge Roll. The gunman turns and starts shooting people down the line. A 9-year-old girl waiting in line is hit. 10:11 a.m.: The first 911 call about the shooting is received. The shooter attempts to reload his weapon when a woman grabs the gun's magazine and rips it away from him. The shooter tries to put another magazine in the gun, but the spring in the magazine fails. Two men subdue him until authorities arrive.

It is hoped that this tragedy, that happened in Tucson will help politicians and others to tone down the rhetoric in their dealings with one another, even when they disagree on various subjects. At this point in time doctors are optimistic that Rep. Giffords may have a significant recovery.

The Democrats did not do well at all in the mid-term elections. Therefore many thought that the lame-duck session of Congress would also be a rough time for President Obama. He surprised everyone with a politically successful lame-duck session of Congress.

He was able to get the nuclear pact with Russia, New Start. This is considered by many to be the most significant arms-control agreement in almost two decades. The tax deal the president was able to negotiate with Republican leaders was remarkable. Even though many Liberal Democrats continued to complain. Economists agreed that the deal he made with Republicans to extend the Bush-era tax cuts would speed economic growth.

The president also was able to get the "don't ask don't tell" policy repealed, which was also one of his campaign promises.

The president concluded that this was "the most productive post-election period we've had in decades" and "the most productive two years that we've had in generations."

Another revolutionary idea and a campaign commitment was to repeal the policy of Don't Ask Don't Tell, for personnel in the military service.

In early December Defense Secretary Robert Gates, according to an article in The Washington Post, wanted the Senate to repeal "don't ask don't tell" before the courts forced him to eliminate the policy.

It seems that Secretary Gates thought that having the change imposed by the courts would be the most disruptive and damaging to military morale and performance.

The Pentagon Working Group's study is the 23rd on the subject of gays in the military. The findings of the group's study: Allowing gay men and lesbians to serve openly would not harm the armed forces. Most of those in uniform services do not think that there will be a great problem adjusting to the change.

There was a Pentagon report of approximately 115,000 respondents, released the end of November 2010. The report was on the policy "don't ask don't tell." The report was considered by many as remarkable because of the respectful way it was handled, especially concerning such a delicate subject. There are many of those surveyed that believe repealing the policy will harm the military. Some personnel in combat units are concerned that gay service members may flaunt their sexuality or engage in inappropriate behavior if the policy is repealed.

There are already regulations that prohibit inappropriate sexual relationships and behavior, which are grounds for punishment regardless of sexual orientation.

Military leaders believe that they can integrate gays just as they did with blacks and women.

President Obama, Defense Secretary Robert M. Gates and Adm. Mike Mullen, Chairman of the Joint Chiefs of Staff support repeal, but some on Capital Hill are still uncomfortable with the idea of change. They should listen to Defense Secretary Gates who indicates that this is a decision that should be made by lawmakers and military officials, not the courts.

After more that 17 years, the president and others are ready to repeal a law or policy that was enacted during President Clinton's presidency.

Mrs. Obama greeted injured service members, their families and guests, who attended the dedication ceremony of the first of three completed Fisher House homes at the National Naval Medical Center in Bethesda, Maryland. The Fisher House Foundation provides housing for families of patients receiving medical care at military and Veterans Affairs hospitals. This organization is among 10 charities that President Obama chose to support with his Nobel Peace Prize money. Fisher House received the largest share, $250,000, most of which helped pay for the construction.

Passage of the repeal will fulfill a campaign promise of President Obama, to end this unfair requirement of gay personnel serving in the Armed Forces. Supporters of the repeal had hoped it could be repealed while Democrats still controlled the Congress. Conservatives were saying there was no reason to rush passage of the repeal, without a full debate of the issue.

The president hoped to win back some of the independent voters, by showing his willingness to compromise. His liberal supporters were furious about President Obama's decision to extend all of President Bush's era tax cuts. White House officials said that was part of a strategy to show President Obama's willingness to compromise. The strategy came about after hours of post-election meetings of senior administration officials, who after going over returns, exit polls and midterm history have determined that the loss of independent voters who supported in 2008 cost the party dozens of races this year. That conclusion placed Obama at odds with many liberal Democrats who say the midterm losses were the result of the president's willingness for compromise.

The GOP was unified, so President Obama did not get what he really wanted, which was to end Bush tax cuts on all household incomes over $250,000. Instead he went along with Republicans to extend the top-tier cuts for two years in exchange for unemployment insurance and other measures intended to boost the economy. The president was trying to make the best of a bad situation, according to Administration officials, who say that restoring the president's image as a post-partisan leader is more important for the next two years of his term.

President Obama delivered a sharp rebuke to Democrats who said they would rather let tax rates rise for everyone than continue perks for millionaires.

> "I am not willing to let working families across this country become collateral damage for political warfare here in Washington," he said. "The American people didn't send us here to wage symbolic battles or win symbolic victories."

Republicans embraced the agreement.

On Tuesday, December 7, 2010 President Obama faced angry Democrats who strongly opposed his deal with Republicans on tax cuts. The Obama and GOP compromise will extend all the tax cuts that were set to expire December 31, 2010 including for the wealthiest households; continue long-term unemployment benefits through the end of next year; give businesses a major tax break to encourage capital investment; and provide working couples as much as $4,200 in extra cash in 2011 through a one year payroll tax.

The far-reaching package will add more than $900 billion to the deficit over the next two years, according to economists.

The $858 Billion tax plan negotiated by the White House and Republican leaders went through the Senate without a problem on Wednesday, 15 December 2010 and is headed for a vote in the House on Thursday as lawmakers rush to prevent a New Year's tax hike for every American household.

During the November elections of 2010, Republicans gained control of the House of Representatives. Many believed that this great victory for the Republicans was because of the support given several freshmen politicians by a group of citizens referred to as the "Tea Party". It appears that we not only have a House of Representatives with a Republican majority, it is as though we have two separate Houses of Representatives: It's as though the Speaker has to have counsel with two separate groups in his own party before he makes his decisions.

I don't think there has ever been a previous time when a group of freshmen congressmen have had so much influence on decisions made by The House of Representatives. It is possible that is why it was so difficult for the House and the Senate to reach a compromise in their efforts to prevent a Government shut-down in April 2011.

Citizens can only hope that the two major bodies of our government can find ways of dealing with the more serious problems of our country other than political posturing. It appears that most voters want the House and Senate to work together and agree on the best solutions to the problems or situations they have to consider.

It appears that the economy is improving according to the stock market and the unemployment rate is down to 8.8%. It is possible that the Obama administration will continue to amaze us with many improvements in the government and the country.

The revolutionary image of President Obama's campaign and election began with the campaign. It was managed differently from any other in recent history. The way the campaign was able to use the internet to get their message out and raise money was so successful that they were able to refuse government finance. The campaign was also able to recruit young people to become involved in the election process. The campaign was able to evaluate the action of the opposition and prepare an effective response.

There were so many challenges faced by President Obama that were never a problem for previous candidates. They were revolutionary because no other candidate for president had been faced with the same problems or had faced the same type of accusations made about them.

There was the incident about the church that the Senator and his family attended. There were controversies about the minister, Rev. Wright. This should have had no effect on Senator Obama's campaign but it continued to a point that he and his family resigned from the church's membership.

So the question of the church and the minister became a non issue after awhile. The strange and shocking accusations that followed were that Senator Obama was a Muslim. It was as though some people were determined to find an issue that would sabotage the Senator's campaign. It is not a routine problem for a candidate to be questioned about the church he or she attends. The Senator stated that he was a Christian. It was thought someone in opposition to the Senator being elected just wanted to place a negative image of any kind in the public's mind, hoping it would cost the Senator votes. That is why I believe not many people took him seriously when he announced he was running for president. Here was a black man raised by a white Christian family, his grandparents. He was the child of a white mother and a black father from Africa.

Many people just saw the Senator as a black American with a dream whose time had not come, but after reading and listening to reports about the man, I somehow came to the conclusion that the campaign and election of Barack Obama is really an American Revolutionary of words, ideas and of change.

It is also revolutionary that President Obama's election has created one of the largest fields of contenders for the 2012 election. Many people, who thought they had to wait to acquire more experience and maturity, seem to feel that if President Obama could be elected so can they. I hope that many of the future hopefuls are not overlooking the special abilities and qualifications of President Obama. There is something special about the man and his way of relating to people at all levels and ages. He really envisioned a better and greater America. The President has been able to energize people politically who have been inactive for years.

President Obama has been able to get our troops out of Iraq and, according to the Secretary of Defense, we will begin removing our troops out of Afghanistan in July of 2011, as President Obama promised.

President Obama made a great choice of Joe Biden as his Vice President, who is excellent in foreign policy and in dealing with members of Congress. He is also very good with the general public.

President Obama had many negative accusations made against him. Some were expected during bad economic periods, and especially high unemployment. Many presidents have had some of those complaints during their time in office, but no other president, to my knowledge has ever been accused of not being an American citizen after being in office. President Obama was even asked to make his birth certificate public by an envious critic. This could also be considered racist, because President Obama is also the first black American President.

There could not be a greater story to end this writing with, than the news that Osama bin Laden has been killed. Another one of President Obama's hopes was that Osama bin Laden would be captured or terminated soon and that he would do everything he could to make it happen.

President Obama announced on Sunday May 1, 2011, that Osama bin Laden had been killed in a U.S. Operation in Pakistan. This was a great accomplishment for America and the families of those lost in the Attack on America, September 11,

I believe that President Obama will go down in history as one of our greatest presidents of the United States who is also a great statesman.

It is kind of strange that during the eight years that a Republican president was in office, no Republican proposed a health care bill. It seems that would have been the best time to try to get a republican proposed plan accepted and passed.

After the election of President Obama and his Health Care Bill Proposal, Republicans are saying they have a better plan. Most had no desire to try and work on changes of President Obama's plan; they just wanted to prevent it from passing.

It is understandable that some changes in programs for seniors and other entitlement programs may require some changes. Therefore, both Republicans and Democrats should be willing to work together to agree on the best solution.

It is very difficult for a lay person to understand, why most of the conservatives say taxes should not be increased on the wealthiest because they provide jobs. If that's true why is the unemployment rate so high and has been for some time. Maybe people in those groups no longer make the type of investments that create jobs. Maybe they just buy more things and protect their wealth for their families. It is also strange that there was not all the talk about control of spending during the last President's two terms. Now it is the primary topic about what is needed by the government. It seems that this administration has been trying to correct some past problems. It also seems that the Obama Administration is sincere in acknowledging the past service of military personnel and their families. I hope that this administration can help solve a problem of the past for Veterans with disabilities. Our military personnel have always done what is asked of them, to insure our freedom, peace and safety. That is why when they have medical disabilities, the process of awarding medical compensation should not be one of red tape rules, confusion, delay and most of all, disappointment. I hope that this problem can be corrected so our service members, who are now serving, won't have the same problem that Vietnam Veterans have. Some are still trying to get benefits that they rightfully deserve. It is hard to determine where the problem is. We don't know if it is the processing procedure or the evaluating stage of the claim. It takes too long because the Vietnam War has been over many years and most Veterans of that war are in their sixties and seventies, and some are still waiting for a determination on their disability claim. This is outrageous, for people who have put their lives on the line for their country. I hope that the present administration with the help of Congress can correct this problem and homelessness for future Veterans. That would really be a revolutionary conclusion to a serious situation for many Veterans, past and present.

The search for Osama Bin Laden had been in progress for some time. There was a reward of one million dollars for his capture or death. On May 1, 2011 President Obama authorized a government operation that led to the death of Osama Bin Laden. This action was treated as a routine military action, rather than the death of the man who, it is said, was responsible for the 9-11 attack on our country.

If this had happened during any other President's administration, I believe there would have been a much larger celebration of the incident. This man's death also caused a great disruption in the operation of Al-Qaeda, an enemy of our military and any interest of the United States of America. This was truly a revolutionary action. The anniversary of the 9-11 attack is approaching and it will be interesting to see how much credit will be given for the extermination of Bin Laden.

The President came up with another revolutionary idea before the campaigning of the 2012 President election begins. On 8 September 2011, President Obama presented a $447 billion job creation plan to Congress.

The unemployment rate seems to be stuck at 9%. President Obama presented a package of tax cuts for employers and employees, spending on schools and roads, and to states to keep teachers in jobs and assistance for the unemployed. The President stated that the plan had more tax cuts than new spending. He also included enlarging a tax cut to provide $1,500 in savings for the average family. He included another tax cut for businesses that hire new employees. The President said, "the purpose of the American Jobs Act is simple: to put more people back to work and more money in the pockets of those who are working. It will provide a jolt to an economy that has stalled and give companies confidence that if they invest and hire, there will be customers for their products and services." The President's plan would subsidize employment for young workers as well as poor workers. It seems that the president believes that this Job Plan will reduce the unemployment rate and also help home owners by making refinancing loans available at record low rates. It is hoped that the Congress and the President will be able to work together for the good of the country as a whole. They may discover that it is the best politics for both parties and a refreshing change.

Bibliographical Notes

The following are some of the sources I used for this writing. I hope they will help explain my point of view, that Senator Obama's campaign and election was an American Revolution.

#1—http://en.wikipedia.org/wiki/United_States_presidential_election,_2008_timeline

AARP Bulletin

American Encyclopedia, International Edition.

The Audacity of Hope. Barack Obama

AARP—BULLENTIN March 2009

AARP—BULLENTIN March 2010

Dreams from my Father. Barack Obama

Obama: The Historic Campaign in Photographs. Deborah Willis and Kevin Merida

Essence Magazine—Special Collector's Edition: 56 page tribute, January 2009

Barack Obama's Road to the Whitehouse 60 Minutes DVD—Steve Kroft

The Charlie Rose Show (DVD)

http://en.wikipedia.org/wiki/
United_States_presdential_election

United State Presidential Election 2008 Timeline

Time Magazine (person of the year issue). December
29, 2008 / January 5, 2009.

*President Barack Obama—The man and his
Journey.*—This special journey where one man
inspires us to change the world and encourages
us with the constant refrain—Yes we Can! (DVD
October 25, 2009)

Special Commemorative Calendar 2009—The South
Brooklyn Book Company

HuffingtonPost.com—May 2009

Following Editions of *The Washington Post*
newspaper were used as sources.

2009

January 20, 2009	Things that Occurred During Obama's Year of Birth
May 1, 2009	HuffingtonPost.com
June 25, 2009	Role of First Lady
December 23, 2009	Health Care Bill
December 23, 2009	First Year Recovery / Economy
December 25, 2009	Senate Democrats Approved Health Care Legislation Christmas Eve

2010

January 20, 2010	Election of Scott Brown (Edward Kennedy's Vacancy) Martha Coakley was Democratic Candidate
January 20, 2010	20 Yr. Old From Bethesda, MD 61 Month Jail Term for Plot to Kill President Obama
April 23, 2010	President Obama to New York Meet w/ Financial Exc.—Financial Reform

April 23, 2010	Speech on Financial Sector
May 10, 2010	Selection of Elena Kagan Supreme Court
June 21, 2010	President Obama—Ref. Fathers for Father's Day
June 22, 2010	President Obama Met with Insurance Exc. of Major Insurance Companies Ref. Raising Premiums
June 23, 2010	Problems with Combat in Afghan.—Talk of the Possibility of General Stanley McChrystal being fired
August 7, 2010	Ref. Stimulus Pkg.
August 7, 2010	Ref. American Health Ins.
August 11, 2010	
August 18, 2010	Some of President Obama's Promises Coming to Pass

Week of August 19, 2010

August 31, 2010	President Eco. Team Discussing Ways to Bolster Growths and Improve Job Opportunities
August 31, 2010	President Obama Declares U.S. War in Iraq Over
September 1, 2010	Iraq War Over
September 22, 2010	Ref. Bob Woodward's Book—Way Out of Afghanistan in 2009
October 8, 2010	Ref. Federal Workers—Working At Home
November 3, 2010	Midterm Election Very Difficult for President Obama and Democrats
November 14, 2010	Ref. President Obama Being a One-Term President
December 1, 2010	Mtg. President Obama and Republicans to Reach Agreement on the Tax Cuts Due to Expire End of 2010

December 1, 2010	Another Campaign Promise was to Repeal the Policy "Don't Ask Don't Tell"
December 3, 2010	Ref. Tax Cuts
December 3, 2010	Mrs. Obama Greeting Injured Service Members and Their Families
December 7, 2010	President Willing to Compromise
December 17, 2010	
December 18, 2010	Don't Ask Don't Tell
December 19, 2010	
December 23, 2010	
December 31, 2010	Financial Crisis Began on Wall Street—Risky Mortgages, etc.
December 31, 2010	Eco Growth

2011

| January 6, 2011 | Harry Reid (D-Nev.) still Leader of Senate |

January 6, 2011   Republican Gain
                         Control of The House of
                         Representatives

January 10, 2011

January 20, 2011